Amazon FBA

Reselling Strategies For More Income on FBA

By: Argena Oivis

www.ArgenaOlivis.com

Download Your Amazon FBA Bundle Creation Course + Video On How To Get Approved In Gated Categories

In the Amazon bundles mini course you'll learn how to create bundles for Amazon FBA, which leads to a more stable business model and less competition.

Also, get our free video on how to get approved in categories. You'll need this this to take your business to the next level.

http://www.argenaolivis.com/fbaeBook

Table Of Contents

Introduction

Congratulations for taking time out of your schedule to further your Amazon Business. There are a million things you can be doing but instead you decided to read *"Amazon FBA: Reselling Strategies For More Income On FBA"*.

As you already know, there's millions of buyers on Amazon because it's a trusted channel. It like Google for buyers, people go there looking to spend money. They have credit cards on file. So let's make the buy button your best friend.

I'm assuming you're not a beginner. This book is for those who are already selling on Amazon but wants to take their business to the next level. Everyday, new people are finding out about reselling on Amazon and are taking action on reselling.

This means increased competition, but with the strategies we'll cover in the book, you'll be able to start working smarter. It's time to take your business to the next level by creating products or bundles that allow you to have more control over your income and your business.

With millions of listings that are already created on Amazon, you can go to a store, scan a product and see how it's selling. You send it to the fulfillment center and once it gets there, the price can drop significantly by new sellers coming in and trying to list this item at the lowest price point possible.

This has happened to many, if not all of us that have been selling on FBA for a while. Something may seem like a good choice, but the listing can become less profitable at anytime and there's nothing you can do but wait.

But you don't want to wait because that leads to long term

storage fees and eventually you may just want to lower to price to get it out of the warehouse.

This book goes into creating a business that you can have control over with the following strategies: multipacks, bundles, wholesale, private label, and online arbitrage. It also goes into how to create listings that will sell your product and how to market the products to get more eyeballs on it.

I know you've heard this before but reading is not enough, you can't just read this book and say it didn't work or that the information wasn't useful if you don't put it into action.

Be mindful and actually put this information into action and get some results with these strategies before doubting that they'll work. The most successful business owners take action and use the information they're given before doubting the process.

I know that you have what it takes to create an income worth bragging about if you just stick with it and give it all you've got.

Thanks again for downloading the book, I truly appreciate it.

Chapter 1: Multipacks

With regular listings on Amazon you're able to go to a retail store, find a product that's already listed, and then send that single product into Amazon. You also have the option to send more than one of that item into Amazon and sell them as a single unit.

But multipacks allow to get some leverage and stand out from all the other competing sellers for that product.

A mulitpack is having 2 or more of the same item in a single listing. This means the customer would not need to order two or more of the same item, but they simply buy multiples of that item for one particular price.

This in turn saves the customer money and time. They won't have to worry about reordering the product so often on Amazon if they buy a multipack of the item.

It also saves you money in Amazon Fees. Amazon charges fees per product and technically a mulitpack listing will be only one product.

This method gives you leverage because you are thinking ahead, this will also get you more income per item. And if you can list the multipack for $25 or more they will qualify for super saver shipping. Customers love this because they can get their items shipped to them earlier and save.

You can do multipack listings in the health and beauty category and in the grocery category. If you're not yet approved for these categories make sure to scroll down to the end of this book and get your free category approval video.

So let's get right into the process. The first thing you do

is log into your seller account and go to **inventory >
add a product.**

Next click on the button that says "create a new product".

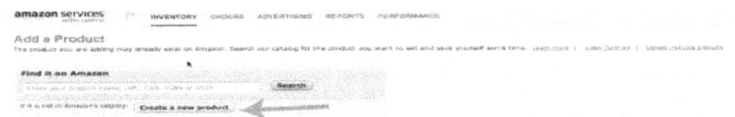

Then select the category of item that you want to sell the
multipack in. Keep in mind that only certain categories
allow you to create multipacks. The main ones are health
and beauty and groceries.

So, select the category that best fits the item you will be
selling.

Then you'll end up on the product listing screen.

If you are selling a multipack for a product that's already listed on Amazon you can simply copy and paste most of the information for that listing since it's basically the same item.

Everywhere you see a red asterisk (*) you need to fill out that field in order for your listing to be accepted.

Product name: Copy and paste the name from the original listing into this box. Make sure to add the words "pack of ____" at the end. Make sure to emphasize the number of items in your mulitipack.

For example: Jolly Rancher Candy Assorted Flavors (Pack Of 3)

Brand Name: This is where you add the brand of the item you're selling. For example: General Mills, Equate, and Colgate are brand names.

Package Quantity: Make sure you put the number of items that are included in your multipack. <u>Do not leave this blank</u> or Amazon will think it's a single item.

EAN or UPC: If you're selling an item that's already listed on Amazon, you can use the same UPC code from the original listing of the item begin sold.

But, if this is the first time this item will be listed on Amazon you'll need to buy UPC codes. You can get a ton of UPC codes for cheap on Ebay. Search eBay for "Amazon UPC codes".

The rest of the information on this page is not necessary to fill out, but if you want to you can. It never hurts to include extra details about the product.

Now, click the "next" button at the end of the page or click on the tab that says "Other".

Condition: Add the item condition, if you're selling in the health and beauty or in the grocery categories the item must be in new condition to send it FBA.

Your Price: Add the price you'll be selling the multipack for. It's up to you what you feel should be the best price, but if the customer is buying a multipack they'd like to save a few dollars by buying more at one time.

It's great if you can get the price $25 or more so they can qualify for the super saver shipping.

For example: If an item is selling for $10 by itself and you want to do a multipack of 3. You can price your item as high as $30. But you may want to knock off $2-$5 to make the listing more appealing. I would sell that mulitpack for between $25-$27.

Quantity: Add the number of items in your mulitpack.

Shipping Method: Choose the radio button that says "I want Amazon to ship and provide customer service for my items if they sell".

Okay, you're finished with this section. Now click on the tab that says "Images".

Images: If the item you're creating a multipack for is

already on Amazon, you're able to use the image from that original listing. You do not have to take your own images unless the product is not yet listed on Amazon.

So if it is already listed, simply go over to that listing and right click on the image you want to use and save it to your computer. Then upload it to the listing that you're in the process of creating.

If you have to take your own images, make it on a white background. You only need an image of the product you're selling-- not an image of the multiple items in your mulitpack.

For example: If you're selling 3 packs of markers. You don't need to take a picture of the three packs of markers, just one pack of markers.

So once you have your image, click on the button that says "add image" and find the image file on your computer and upload it. You're able to list up to 7 pictures. So if you want to show the item from multiple angles (front, back, sides, ect.) then you can do so. But you're only required to have one. But keep in mind the more you have the better for the customer. Images must be 1000x500 pixels.

Description: You can copy and paste what's in the description for the other listing if there's already one created. If not, you'll have to create your own.

Key Product Features: You get five lines where you get to talk about your product's features. Features are your products' most important qualities and this information will be displayed as bullet points in your listing. Make sure you tell the customer the exact the number of the product they'll be receiving in one of those bullet points.

Product Description: You have a 2,000 character

max to explain your product in a general manner (not particularly the item).

Tip: Go to Google and search for Amazon best sellers and take a look at the listings there so you can get some ideas of what a good product description and features are.

Keywords: None of these fields are necessarily required but you do want to make sure you fill out the search terms so people will find your item. Unless, the item is already listed. If it's already listed just copy and paste.

If you have to come up with your own search terms, make sure you're thinking into the mind of the buyer. If you were searching for your item what would you type into the Amazon search bar? Those are the words you want to be using. Use descriptive words that people will likely be searching for.

The search terms and keywords are extremely important because this is how customers will be able to find your listing when shopping.

More Details: Here, you just fill in as much information as possible. The more the better.

Product dimensions: This is something you can't simply copy and paste because you have to measure your entire multipack's dimensions. Amazon needs to know this information because they like to know what size box to use in advance when packaging items. What I usually do is measure the dimensions using a tape measurer. You're going to need the products' length, height, and width.

Weight: Weigh the product using an appropriate scale. You can round up, but do not round down. If you haven't yet gotten a scale here is a checklist of the items you'll need to run your FBA business: http://www.argenaolivis.com/wp-content/uploads/2014/10/fbachecklist.pdf

Number of Items: Put the number of items that is included in your multipack.

Unit Count: Put the number of items that is included in your multipack.

Unit Count Type: Put down the material your product comes in (example: bag, bottle, jar, box, ect.)

Okay, once you're done filling in as much information as you can make sure you click on the button that says "save and finish". Next you'll come to the screen and you'll see your products' ASIN number, image, sku, and title.

You won't be able to view the listing right away. The typical wait is about 15 minutes. Once you check out the new listing, you should see on your image that Amazon has put an image that says how many of the item there is.

For example: If you have a 5 pack. Amazon should have a logo and sticker on your picture that says "5 pack". This makes it official.

So now you're done. You've created your multipack. Now all

you need to do is send it off to Amazon.

Make sure when you send the multipack in that you have something that can hold these items together. Either a clear poly bag or stretch wrap will do. If you're using a poly bag make sure to include a suffocation label. Also, make sure you have a sticker on each multipack that says "sold as set, do not separate".

Chapter 2: Bundles

In this chapter we're going to go into exactly how to create a bundle for Amazon FBA. Bundles are a great way to actually stand out from the competition. It's a chance to be more creative and to take a chance to see if you can put yourself in the mind of the consumer.

A bundle is when you package 2 or more related products together.

With bundles you have to think about what customers would buy together. You can do bundles for holidays or just for things that would sell well together all year around.

To get my free mini course on how to create bundles make sure to visit:
http://www.argenaolivis.com/bundlecreationcourse

Keep in mind that bundles are much different from multipacks because you'll be doing all the leg work and it's just like creating your own product. But it's totally worth it, because it puts you in a place where you have more control over your business.

It also makes it harder to get intruders on your listing that will drive the price down. If you source your products from different locations or use copyrighted items, your bundle is unlikely to be bombarded by sellers who can bring down the price.

So, first thing first. You're going to need an idea of what you want to create a bundle on.

Great bundles are ones with items that truly complement each other; something where you can't have one without the other.

For example: a coffee mug and coffee. Or coffee and creamer. Things like this are obvious, but they work.

Just think. Think about gifts. Think about holidays or seasons that are approaching. Think about different niches (weddings, golf, biking).

Think about what you'd buy as a bundle. If you need some inspiration, go into retail stores and grocery stores and start putting together some things in the aisle.

Also, use Amazon. Search amazon for the word "bundle" and see what's out there to get some ideas. If you're looking to sell in a particular category, do your search for bundles in that category. Another trick is to start typing in your keywords on Amazon to and see what search results they suggest without even finishing the entire search.

For example: search Amazon for Valentines Day Bundle and see what shows. Or search Amazon for wedding bundle. Make sure you're searching in the correct departments.

So now I'm assuming you've done your research and made sure that whatever you want to create a bundle on that there's a market for it. Are people buying the items that you want to sell in your bundle separately, if so, you're good to go. You can tell if an item is selling a few a day if it has a rank below 100,000.

Keep in mind also, the size of the products that you're thinking of bundling together. You don't want them to be too big because of Amazon's oversize storage fees. And the more the product weighs, the more you'll be paying in shipping costs.

Make sure that whatever products you use to put your bundles together that they'll be readily available again if you need to replenish them.

So let's get started. I'm assuming you have gotten an idea and went out to buy the materials for your bundles. You should send at least 10 bundles to FBA to start off with. If they do well, you can always send in more.

But let's test out this bundle first. And I hope you're ready put put in some leg work.

So, since you'll technically be creating a new product on Amazon, you're going to need a UPC code for your bundle. You can get these very inexpensively on eBay and other sites.

So, log in your seller account and follow the same process for setting up your new listing as you did with the multipack in Chapter 1.

Since we've already went into how to do most of this in Chapter 1, I'm just going to get into the most important things that should definitely be included in your listing.

Product Name: The name should stand out and you can get creative in what you call the bundle. Use your main keywords. This is also a great place to describe the item (color, size, etc.) Make sure you add the word "bundle" too.

Price: Make sure to price your bundle to where you're making a profit. Do the math and see how much you'll be paying in Amazon fees for each item. If your bundle sells well at a certain price, keep increasing the price until you see that no one is buying it.

You need to see the highest someone is willing to pay so you can earn the maximum. You don't want to overcharge, and keep in mind that if your bundle is $35 or more that customers will be eligible for the free 2 day shipping.

Try your best to keep the margins of the items you're bundling together low so you can make more profit per bundle.

Product Image: Make sure to include everything that's included in your bundle in the main picture. In the additional pictures you can add an image of each product separately.

The main image should have a white background and look appealing to the eye. Do the best you can to angle all the products in your image so that they look professional and clean. The better the image looks, the more sales you're likely to get.

Cameras

As far as cameras go. No need to go out and buy anything fancy; the camera from your smart phone or from a tablet will suffice. Or you can use a digital camera.

Background

You want to make sure there's nothing in the background when you are taking pictures. So make sure you either get a back drop or use poster boards to create a background. I personally use poster-boards.

If you still can't seem to remove the background from your images, there are photo editing tools that you can use to remove the background from your images.

A free one is picmonkey.com-- to access the tool to remove the background visit www.Pickmoney.com and click edit> upload image from computer > effects (on the left sidebar) > scroll down and click on the "draw" box. There you can erase the background. There are also paid services that make it much easier such as Clipping Magic and Bonanza.

Lighting

As far as lighting goes, the best type of light to have is natural light but the problem with this is obvious. There can be weather issues and issues with background. If you can't get outside try to get near a very big window. Or you can invest in a nice photography lighting kit.

So basically, when it comes to your product images, work with what you already have on hand and try your best to create the most quality and professional looking pictures that you can and you should be fine.

Packaging Bundles

The best way by far to package bundles is to use clear poly bags. When using a clear poly bag, make sure you put a sticker on there that says "sold as set, do not separate".

Also, don't forget your suffocation label. You also have the option to send them in boxes, but it gets costly if you have to buy a ton of boxes. Same as the bag, make sure to put a sticker on there that says "sold as set, do not separate".

Reviews

You have technically just created a whole new product so you're going to need to get reviews. The best way to do this is to use Amazon ads to get tons of eyeballs on your bundle.

When you have a professional account you're able to put your product on sale or offer a discount code. Create discount codes for your family members, friends, email list, or audience and let them know that you're trying to get reviews.

So basically, you know everything you need to know about creating a successful bundle on Amazon. Now it's time for you to take some action and start sending some bundles into Amazon sooner than later.

Chapter 3: Wholesale

Wholesale is another way to have some control over your Amazon FBA business. By doing wholesale you're able to cut down on the amount of work you have to do.

The idea here is to find a product that you know will sell very well and contact the manufacturer of the product and get a bunch sent to you, label them and list them, the send them off to the fulfillment center.

You get to list a bunch of the same products and all you have to do is change the quantity amount before sending to Amazon.

Before you do wholesale though, there are a few things you'll need in order to start:

Become a legal business:

Make sure you become a legal business such as a LLC or Corporation depending on your country so the wholesale companies that you'll be reaching out to will take you seriously.

If wholesale companies see you as another "individual seller" just trying to resell, they may test you and tell you that you need to order a ton of products up front to make sure you're serious about this.

And you never want to order tons and tons of products; you really want to see how they'll do first before you invest tons on money.

You can become a legal company by applying in your state. Fees may vary.

EIN Number/Federal Employer Identification Number

Once you become a legal business you'll need an EIN number. An EIN number stands for Employer Identification Number. An EIN number is similar to a social security number that you can use to identify your business for legal, business, and tax reasons. You get this number by filing with the IRS or whatever the governing body is for your country.

Wholesale License

There are many names for what this is called. Different states call it different things. It's also known as a reseller's certificate, sellers permit, and a permit license. This license allows you to purchase wholesale and resell. When you have this license, vendors do not charge sales tax on the items you purchase.

Keep in mind to check with your state and country to make sure you have all the license and permits you need to wholesale on Amazon.

Tax ID Number

You will also need to apply for a tax ID number in addition to an EIN. This allows you to charge taxes to people that buy your products. There is no fee for this, but it may vary by state/country.

Okay, so now that you have all your legal stuff set up it's time to get started wholesaling on Amazon.

So just like with bundle and multipack creation, we want to make sure we do our market research and find a product that 's already selling. The best way to determine the market you want to get into is to use Amazon and Alibaba.com as search engines.

Go to Amazon and type in something that you may be interested in selling. The best way to find products is to go to Google and type in "Amazon Best Sellers" and look in the different categories on Amazon and see what's selling.

You don't want to go after something that's too trendy. Look for things that you know people will be interested in buying for years to come. Once you find an item that looks interesting, do a separate search for it in the Amazon search bar.

Look for the following: the amount of reviews, the sales rank, and the price it's selling for. See how many reviews the product has, if the product doesn't have a ton of reviews then you may be able to compete.

Look at the sales rank, if it's below 100,000 that means its selling a few a day, which is not bad at all. But the sales rank varies by categories because some categories have more products than others.

Finally, look at the price it's selling for. You don't want to sell anything below $12 on FBA, because of fees. You don't want the Amazon fees to cut too deeply into your profits. Also, look for the listings that have the prime symbol next to them because you'll be in a whole different market when selling through FBA.

The listings without the prime symbols are being merchant fulfilled so you have to keep in mind that many customers will want to buy through prime to save on shipping and they know that the products are coming straight from the fulfillment center. And most customers don't even know that there are individual resellers on Amazon through FBA.

Now, go over to Alibaba.com and type in the same product you're researching on Amazon and type in the product name and see how much the typical manufacturer will want you to pay per item. Compare the price you'll be paying per unit to what the product is typically selling for on Amazon.

You want to be able to sell the product for at least three times your money for it to be worthwhile for you.

Keep in mind that there are tons of websites where you can buy wholesale items from. Or if you see a product that looks profitable, you may want to do your research and find the manufacturer of the product and contact the manufacturer directly.

Also, look for loop holes like bundling 2 or 3 items together, being creative like this will help you to stick out from the other listings.

Contacting The Manufacturer

Make sure you're professional when you send the manufacturer a message. You want to ask questions that make you look professional and do not let them know that you're new to wholesaling. This is why you did all the extra work to make yourself look professional like setting up a phone number, website, and having your proper licenses.

You ultimately want to build a relationship with the manufacturer, don't think of buying from them as a one time thing. Once you establish a relationship they'll be able to trust you and will be willing to work with you. You want them to work with you so you can get a lower price per item and can come to them if there's anything wrong with the shipment.

When you're first starting out you may want to try contacting local manufacturers. You can filter your search on Alibaba so that you're only looking at manufacturers that are closer to you.

When contacting them, kindly ask for a sample. They may

send you one for free or may ask you to pay shipping. Ask them about the different colors and other variations the product may have.

You truly want to research the product as thoroughly as possible. Take weight, price, color, and variations of the product into consideration.

You also want to ask them about warranties, and what will happen if something happens to the shipment when buying a large quantity. Ask them what will happen if one or all of the products that were sent to you either didn't work or were damaged upon arrival.

Make sure that all the conversations between you and the manufacturer are recorded or saved, so you can refer back to it just in case something goes down.

Also, take screen shots of the product you'll be investing in just in case the manufacturer tries to change any information on their page or website. Get all the proof you can and save it in a folder on your desktop.

When just starting out, try not to buy too many quantities of an item your first time around. Be conservative and try to make the one product work first before moving on. This way you can analyze any mistakes and apply what you learned to the next wholesale batch.

Also, look at different deal websites where you can buy products at a really low price without having to specific quantity you have to invest in. These sites are out there. Alibaba is not the only place to look for wholesale items.

By starting off with these deal sites you won't have the same requirements you'd need when contacting serious manufacturers. You may just want to test the water and set some things up for now until you're able to get all the proper business licenses.

Be extra cautious when ordering products from overseas and keep in mind that products will take a while to arrive.

Make sure to use the same techniques that you used when creating your own listings for bundles when creating your product pages for your wholesale items.

Sending Your Products In

Depending on how good of a deal you found, you may find that you got 500-1000 products shipped to you. You do not want to send them all in at once. I suggest you send in 100 or so to test out the market.

By sending in only 100, you get to see how the product will sell. If you see it's not selling you can create a mulitpack out of the product so it can stand out or you can do other things like bundle it with something.

Also, if you're only selling a few a day, you don't want to get stuck with long term storage fees which happen yearly. So make sure your product is selling the way you want it to before sending them all in.

And with all this information, you're ready to start selling wholesale. Take action and you can build a business that you have more control over and where you can expect a steady stream of income.

Once you learn how to market your listings and how to choose the right products at the best price, you'll stick out from the crowd and earn much more money.

Even if you're not successful at first but you take action, you're still ahead of the person still on the couch watching TV or playing video games. Take your business seriously and build it up now so that later you won't have to work as hard later.

Chapter 4: Private Label

There's been a lot of talk, and frankly, a lot of hype about private labeling products on Amazon.

Let me tell you this now, it's not easy and it'll take a large investment of both time and money to get your product off the ground.

Private labeling products for Amazon FBA is basically when you get a product that can be massed produced and be re-branded and you create your own brand around that product to make it "different" from the others.

You would make your product different by changing something small like the logo, color, size, or just the brand name of the product.

Private labeling your own products are for those that are serious and are willing to go to the next step to make more income on FBA. It's not for a quick buck, it's for those that want to create a professional brand and build a true business for the future.

So if you're serious about FBA, this may be something you want to get into.

Sourcing for products to private label is pretty similar to looking for products to sell wholesale. You'd basically go through the same process in chapter 3 to analyze the competition and see what market you can get into where there's some competition but you can somehow stand out or "out market" them.

So if you don't know how to analyze the competition to see if the product is a good investment, go back to chapters 2 and 3 and analyze the competition based on keywords, reviews, sales rank, etc.

Some extra tips when looking for the right product to private label is to stay away from seasonal items. Items that only sell in certain seasons are not a good fit because this means your sales will slow down when it's not that particular season.

For example: You may want to stay away from Christmas decorations or swimming pool accessories.

Also, stay away from items that are patented like Ipads and items with sports team logos on them. We're creating our own brand here and you don't want to infringe on anyone's trademark.

For example: Generic products like scissors, water bottles, phone cases, wrist bands, etc. Are some things you **would be able to** private label without a problem.

When looking to sell your products, make sure they will sell for $12 or more. You don't want to sell items that sell for a low price because you have to keep Amazon fees in mind.

Speaking of Amazon fees, make sure you don't pick a product that weighs a lot. You want a product that's light weight (less than one pound) because Amazon will charge you extra to ship out products that are heavier.

Also, keep the size of the product in mind; you can also get oversize fees if your product is too large (too long or big). So make sure it's smaller than 8x8x8 inches.

As far as rank goes, make sure that similar items have a rank of 10,000 or less. When you're getting into your own product you want to make certain that there's a market for it. In some cases a competition can be a good thing. If you're willing "out market" your competition.

How To "Out Market" Your Competition

Out marketing your competition is basically doing a better job at marketing and advertising your product on Amazon. There are many sellers on Amazon that just put up a product but don't truly know how to market.

I'm basically trying to say, be outstanding and go above and beyond when it comes to your product and especially your product listing. Below are some tips:

Images: Make sure your images are professional and makes the consumer want to buy. Use as many pictures as Amazon will allow you to post for that listing.

Research/Keywords: Do research on the keywords you'll use for your listing. You can use free tools such as Google Adwords Keywords Tool or paid tools for more advanced research.

And don't forget about the best search engine there is when looking for keywords: Amazon. Start typing in a keyword and see what options come up in the drop down menu for suggested keywords. These keywords are the ones people are typing into Amazon to find products.

Use related keywords to your main keyword. Put yourself inside the customer's shoes and think about how you would search for your item.

Description: Use html, find a template that you can use to make your description stand out. Use relevant keywords and add as much information as possible. Tell your customer why they should buy from you instead of your competitor. Brush up on your copyrighting skills.

Reviews: Do anything you can to get as many reviews as you can. Many times reviews are the reason someone will buy from you instead of a competitor. If you have a professional account you can create discounts for your customers by creating a promo code.

If you already have an audience/email list that's great because you can ask them to give you an honest review for your product and give them a promo code to purchase the item at a very low price.

Naming Your Brand

When you private label a product you want to have a brand name that encompasses what your business is about. Make sure the name you use is not taken and think about something cool that people will like and relate to. Make sure the name is relevant to what you're selling too.

Packaging/Logo

Some manufacturers will be able to print your logo/brand right on to the product. Depending on the product size and how far you go. You may just want to tag on the product with your logo.

You can have a logo and or packaging designed at places like Fiverr.com, Odesk.com, or Elance.com. You can work with your manufacturer or you can always get the packaging sent to you and put it on yourself before shipping out your products.

Overall, you can definitely be successful with private labeling. Choose your product(s) carefully and make sure to treat it like a true business. Run Amazon ads, out market your competition, and be creative.

None of this comes easy; it takes patience and sometimes luck in choosing the right product. Learn from any mistakes you make and truly make your product into a brand.

Get on some social media channels to get even more customers over to your products. Create an email list, and really help out and add value to anyone who purchases your product or that is a potential customer. Go above and beyond and successful will usually follow.

Chapter 5: Online Arbitrage

Online arbitrage is when you source products online from different websites that give you amazing deals and sell the items you've purchased on Amazon for a significantly higher price.

Websites
There are tons of websites that features deals where you can source for products. Make sure that it's a trusted website. Also, before buying anything do your product research thoroughly by searching for the product on Amazon and looking at its rank, price it's selling for, and reviews.

Make sure to check out all the big box store websites such as:

- Target.com

- Walmart.com

- Macys.com

- Toyrus.com

- Disneystore.com

- CVS.com

- etc.

Then there are websites that have daily deals. When sourcing on these sites see how much the item was previously selling for so you can tell right away if there may be a deal there. Here are some sites to check out:

- fatwallet.com

- bensbargins.com

- nomorerack.com

- ltdcommodities.com

- slickdeals.net

- ebay.com

- etc.

Sometimes even Amazon.com is a good place for online arbitrage. If you know Amazon will run out of stock on a certain item (Amazon usually has lower prices than sellers) and the price will go up, the product may be worth buying the lower price then sending it in to the fulfillment center.

You can do more thorough research on Amazon running out of stock and see how the highest price that the item has sold for by going to camelcamelcamel.com and typing in your product name. You'll then get more data on your item to make a clearer decision.

Benefits Of Online Arbitrage

You're in the comfort of your own home so you don't have to feel rushed or shy when sourcing or researching products. The products come right to your door so you don't have to spend a ton on gas money by driving to different locations.

You get the products sent right to your door so you can label them and send them right over to the fulfillment center. You also have the ability to buy multiples of an item instead of just a few clearance items that are left on a shelf.

You also don't look weird to the cashier checking out all sorts of random products.

Researching Products

Since you'll have a ton of time to research products before buying you're bound to make better decisions.

Make sure to check on Amazon to see how well the products you've found online for sale are profitable.

You'll know if a product is profitable by looking at the sales rank, the number of positive reviews, and the price the product is selling for.

Sales Rank

Sales rank varies depending on categories. For example: There may be more items in the books category than in the home & garden category.

Amazon has its own algorithm and only they truly know all the details about sales rank.

But there are a few things you can do to make sure the item you send in has a good chance of selling fast.

You can type in the name of the product you're searching for and scroll down to see what categories it's listed in. Click on the category and see how many items are in that category by looking at the top of the search results. It'll say how many products are in that particular category.

So you can make a judgment based on how many products are in that category if your item has a good sales rank.

Reviews

Look at the number of positive reviews an item has. If the item has a ton of negative reviews it may be because it's not a good product. Try your best to sell quality products so you'll have less returns. Generally, you should avoid items with less than 3 stars.

Price

See how much an item is selling for and do more extensive research on pricing your product by visiting camelcamelcamel.com and seeing how often Amazon runs out of stock and the highest price that people are willing to pay for it.

Keep the season in mind when looking at prices the product previously sold for. If it's around Christmas time or other holidays, customers tend to spend more money.

Make sure your item will be profitable. A general rule of selling items for three times your money or more with a minimum of $10 will allow you to create sustainable profits.

To see exactly how much you'll make, you can use tools such as the fba calculator or look in your seller central account.

More Tips For Online Arbitrage

Make sure to take action on these tips because they'll truly help you save money and get the best deals at the lowest prices.

Coupons and Promo Codes

Use coupons and promo codes when purchasing items from websites you're shopping through. You can find promo codes for websites by Googling the "name of the website" and "promo codes". You can easily save 5% or more on your entire purchase by finding coupon codes and promo codes online.

Every single penny saved counts. So just take a few seconds to look. You won't always find something, but at least try.

Rebates

Get rebates on items if the website offers them. Make sure to take action and actually get your money back. A lot of people lose money on rebates because they don't feel like turning them in or they forget. Make sure to write in your schedule when the rebate should be returned or do it right away.

Rewards Cards

Rewards card and similar customer points programs can be beneficial. These are popular for big box stores. Make sure you are always signing up for rewards cards to any store you're going to be shopping. It's a great way to save money.

Newsletters

Sign up for newsletters for all the stores you shop. They'll send you coupons, sales, and promo codes. These can definitely come in handy.

If you don't want your personal email being spammed, open a separate email account for your online arbitrage or create a folder and set your email up so emails from the stores goes straight into that folder so they'll be there when you need them instead of being a pain or a distraction.

Seasonal Items

Avoid sending in seasonal items too early. Think about when people will start searching and buying certain items. You can buy seasonal items on clearance, but make sure to send them in at the proper time to avoid fees.

Store the seasonal items you buy somewhere until it's appropriate to send them in. And be careful; don't pass up a profitable item because it's not selling at the time. Do more research on camelcamelcamel.com

Condition Notes

Make your listing stand out by adding condition notes. This separates you from the crowd and will more likely increase your chances of getting the sale over your competition.

You can include benefits that pertain to the item you're sending like: packaged carefully, packaged securely, bubble wrapped, poly bagged, expiration dates, tested.

You can also include an image of the item if it's not new. If you have the opportunity to, take the image. You'll get the sale most of the time when you take the extra time to do this.

Overall, that pretty much sums of online arbitrage. Of course there are sites that can take out the leg work of having to source products online and just give you deals that you can flip. They're usually paid sites but it may be worth it if you don't want to do your own research.

Just take action and learn from your mistakes. Don't let the fear of doing something wrong stop you. Let it be a lesson to you to apply to your business later for success. Sometimes products can flop or they won't sell the way you expected.

Sometimes you just have to take a chance on a product and you never know. Start off with lower priced items (under $5) until you get the hang of it or your budget increases.

Chapter 6: Amazon FBA Success Tips

The following items in this chapter are more advanced and are necessarily needed to run your business. But I decided to add this chapter for those who really want to scale their business and make it a full time income.

Set Up A Business Bank Account

You'll need a EIN and to incorporate your business to get your account set up. The benefits of a business bank account is it allows you to keep your personal finances separate from your business.

Using credit cards for business

I personally don't use credit cards because I feel like if you can't afford it you shouldn't be buying it.

But credit cards can be a way to establish credit in your business. Also, if you know that you'll be able to pay it off but don't have the money right now, it's a great back up plan.

But don't put you or your business into debt! Think smart. I know with Amazon FBA that you'll have to buy a lot of inventory in order to have a consistent income; but don't over extend your credit card. Pay off the full balance monthly. I don't think business is worth getting into debt over. But it's your call.

Liability Insurance Policy

If you're purchasing a lot of wholesale or private labeling products, you may want to look into getting insurance for your business. This will keep you out of trouble if a shipment ever gets lost or something happens to someone that is using your products.

Also keep very good records, emails, and screen shots of items you purchase from wholesalers so you can protect yourself.

Business Address (PO Box -USPS) – Virtual Mailbox

You may want to go further to protect your identity by getting a business address. There will be a small fee for this. You can set up a local P.O. Box by going to USPS.com or you can get a virtual mailbox.

A virtual mailbox is an online mailbox and is a great way to set up a business address quickly. I've personally used www.virtalpostmail.com and they weren't bad, but do your research.

Business Phone Number

A business phone number is optional but does set you apart, especially if you're buying wholesale. You can use free services such as Google Voice.

Business Website

Having a website also sets you apart from competitors. And when you're creating your own brand or looking to do a deal with a wholesaler, a website can set you apart. And it's a great point of contact for customers who may want to reach out to you or your brand.

Here's my tutorial on how to create a wordpress website from scratch: http://www.argenaolivis.com/website/

Storage Of Products

When you have a bunch of products in your home it may get a

little cluttered. That's why it's best to send items in as soon as possible.

But if you only want to send a few hundred in or it's a seasonal item then you may want to consider having a private room or space in your home to store products. Also, consider renting a storage unit.

Be mindful of different temperatures when storing products. Make sure they're packaged correctly so they don't get damaged, dirty, melt, freeze, etc.

Work Space

If you can have a dedicated workspace where you only do work. This will increase your productivity. It also eliminates tons of distractions and allows you to be come more organized.

Taxes

Consult with a CPA or lawyer to see how much you're supposed to be paying in taxes. Keep all receipts and invoices in separate folders. You can use programs like Microsoft Excel to keep record of your business income and expenses.

Taxes can be complicated because you're selling to people all over the world through Amazon, so just make sure to consult with someone so you can know what to expect and how much money to set aside each month.

Productivity

Always look for ways to do things more efficiently. Sometimes it's worth it to pay someone else to do tedious tasks that you know you're not good at.

Outsource what you can. Don't be opposed to using tools that will help you get better results. Some are paid and some are free.

Marketing

Go above and beyond in your listings, in your branding, and in your FBA business in general.

Create an audience around you and your brand (if applicable). Get people on your email list and provide them with extra value.

If you can, begin to make Amazon's customers your customers by doing things others are too lazy or too busy to do. Start working on your business website and other things that will set you apart.

Everyday there are new sellers coming on to Amazon. By marketing the best you will get the best profits and the best results.

Start doing Amazon ads to market your products. Test out campaigns and really learn how to get eyes on your products.

Mindset

Don't let things like negative feedback or little sales get you down. In business you will experience times that are not so fun. Use anything you fail at as feedback and a way to be better next time.

You have to believe in yourself and your products to be successful. Constantly work on your mindset and realize what you're worth. Most people are afraid to get started or take action, don't let that be you.

Think of where you want to be in the future and work toward it. Set goals, get a schedule and make things happen. You know what to do; now it's time to do it.

Keep learning more about Amazon FBA and learn to invest in yourself.

Staying Organized

As I mentioned, keep good records, keep receipts, and make sure your not taking on too many projects at once.

Store your products in appropriate places and label everything you can. Keep notes. Keep a clean work space.

All in all, I know you have what it takes to scale up your business and implement these advanced Amazon FBA strategies into your business. Make sure you work on your mindset daily and take action on all the information you've learned in this book.

Conclusion

I want to take time out again to thank you for buying this book. It's entrepreneurs like you who will change the world. Make sure you work and take every single thing you've learned and get started.

Use one of the methods above and really master FBA, get some results, and move on the next. Don't try to do too much at once, when you're just starting off; try items like bundles or multipacks. Then move on to the more advanced stuff like wholesale and private label.

I hope this book was able to help you to create more income on FBA.

If you enjoyed this book, can you do me a favor and kindly leave a review for it on Amazon?

By leaving a review you'll be giving me feedback on how to improve the book or let me know what I did well on so I can provide more value when updating the book.

Check Out My Other Books

Below you'll find some of my other popular books that are popular on Amazon and Kindle as well. Simply click on the links below to check them out. Alternatively, you can visit my author page on Amazon to see other work done by me.

Fulfillment By Amazon For Beginners: Step By Step Instructions On How To Make An Income On FBA

Email Marketing Machine: Build Relationships, Get Traffic, and Make Money Online

Online Business Mindset: Confidence Building and Personal Development For Internet Marketers

Make Money Online Fast: Step By Step Instructions On How To Work From Home Using Proven Internet Marketing Strategies

Information Products 101: How To Create And Make Money With Information

Affiliate Marketing 101: How To Make Money Online With Other People's Products

If the links do not work, for whatever reason, you can simply search for these titles on the Amazon website to find them.

Download Your Amazon FBA Bundle Creation Course + Video On How To Get Approved In Gated Categories

In the Amazon bundles mini course you'll learn how to create bundles for Amazon FBA, which leads to a more stable business model and less competition.

Also, get our free video on how to get approved in categories. You'll need this this to take your business to the next level.

http://www.argenaolivis.com/fbaeBook